Nest

poems by

Heather Angier

Finishing Line Press
Georgetown, Kentucky

Nest

Copyright © 2016 by Heather Angier
ISBN 978-1-944899-13-4 First Edition
All rights reserved under International and Pan-American Copyright Conventions. No part of this book may be reproduced in any manner whatsoever without written permission from the publisher, except in the case of brief quotations embodied in critical articles and reviews.

ACKNOWLEDGMENTS

Miniature Magazine: "Tuber"
Switchback: "Anger"
Pirenes Fountain: "Aquafina"
Literary Mama: "Pregnant"
Green Hills Lantern: "Compost"
The Poeming Pigeon: "Gobstopper"

Editor: Christen Kincaid

Cover Art: Thomas Broening

Author Photo: James Johnston

Cover Design: Elizabeth Maines

Printed in the USA on acid-free paper.
Order online: www.finishinglinepress.com
also available on amazon.com

Author inquiries and mail orders:
Finishing Line Press
P. O. Box 1626
Georgetown, Kentucky 40324
U. S. A.

Table of Contents

Compost 1
Crossing the Gila 3
Interstate 80 5
Frances 6
Antique 7
Cricket Trick 8
Nature 10
Canaries 11
Anger 12
Gray Wedding Dress 13
Ghost Town 14
Chinese Dairy Hand 15
Psithurism 16
Anniversary 17
Arthur's Drowned— 18
Nest 19
Nell 20
Gobstopper 21
Ink Blot 22
Furniture 23
Rosewild 25
Pregnant 26
Pancreatic Cancer 27
Aquafina© 28
Moving Virginia to Senior Housing 29
Tuber 30

Compost

The camellias are selling it;
each lusty bloom—
a gorgeous heart
throbbing—*love, oh love*

think of it:

wrapped in quiet
moonlight—I trace
your greying sideburns,
the crow's feet stamped
across your face—and listen
to our old, sold hearts
thumping.

Well, what, so what
that flowers fade, drop
one by one, some-
times in pairs,
to the garden below.

This is love, they yell
falling, *love*

think of it:

all those open hearts
on open hearts—heaps
and heaps of them—
eventually raked, shoveled
into bruised, soggy piles

and look at us
all the while
vaguely aware
something lovely
can still grow from it.

Crossing the Gila
c. 1850

Wagon wheels
      starving dogs

oxen—tongues
swollen, over-burdened

     sinking, sinking
Even the sun

swallowed whole—
     the shifting sand

opening hot
   toothless mouths

dreams
are sinking   Bury it all

     to survive—
books, glass bottles

medicine   Mark it—
bones, bones

in stark moonlight
     Reach Camp

Salvation—*swallow*
   soft beans   hot meat

  clear water   *sink*
into beds—bellies

    swollen   twisted
and aching   This

is the moment
my heart

sinks   this is
when he turns back

swallowed
        in blinding wind

holds the shovel
grits his teeth   and digs

Interstate 80

There is a bleak road ahead
sun-beaten and glaring.

There are tire scraps in the ditches
threadbare and strewn.

There are crows careless in Nevada—
each one, a burden perched

in the silent arms of a bent tree.

Frances
c. 1850

By glowing embers
   limp   rabbit   still
gripped, the moon-
       drenched babies
  now asleep
in the stretched
    canvas wagon—
maybe she could hardly
   form the words:
He took the baby,
William! So I aimed—
     maybe her voice
her hands   cracked
            trembled
  like prairie grass
under the catastrophic
         stars—
    maybe he set
down the pelt-
soft   rabbit   gentle
   in the settling
  smoke—maybe
he held her, his own
   trailing hands
       also unsteady

Antique

I think of her sometimes
on certain occasions—

an anniversary, perhaps
when my ring hits

a raised glass with a ting
and our sparkling laughter

holds up the ceiling—or maybe
on a dim autumn night

having cut my finger—
blood catching

under its tight band; the kids
shrill in a hot trade

of Japanese Erasers—and
I can see myself

becoming her, somehow
repeating the same

household tasks—wiping up
breadcrumbs

and vomit. So that
I want to ask her—if she, too,

grew disappointed, in love
with a man who drank

hard. Ah, but there
I am again—standing

in front of that antique
shop in Georgetown, the window-

reflected buses passing me by
while I gaze at its glittery display—

wondering if the ring will fit me
better or worse

than the woman
who had worn it before.

Cricket Trick

And there appeared Emma
    ghost-pale, beside me—
the star-pocked night
    thick with crickets:

It was 1849—she began,
    and all of us hungry.

We crossed the plains—
    Indians watching, put
our iron pot on the fire.
    When it bubbled, they came
closer, threw in fistfuls of crickets.

Well, what?!—she slapped
    her knee, hard.
The next night?! We picked
    dead cricket from our teeth!

Nature

And then there's you, Mr. Shiny-
Shoes and Ms. All-Business. Why

separate yourselves from me?
What's the big hurry?

Fine, fine. You eat with a fork
and say *excuse me.* Come tomorrow,

trapped in the startling
elevator, your wild eyes

will again search mine. It's then—
just another sighing mother

adjusting her leaky bra,
I'll shrug, as if

it doesn't matter,
mouth: *it's okay,*

I can feed you all.

Canaries

That was the screen door—
          rusted hinge,
     sound of visitors.
Juaquin Murieta,
       wanted dead or alive,
stands politely—clears his throat.
         He studies her children
playing with a wet dish towel
         and a wooden spoon.
Handing him a sack of vegetables—
      the widow pretends
she doesn't notice his scar-
       whipped, brooding heart.
The room swells with understanding.
      It is summer and hot.
The children say when he left
     wild roses tamed
           horses collided
and a flock of gold coins
      dropped like yellow birds
to the dusty floor boards below.

Anger

Blown in like a cloud
of billowing pollen—

see how it carries on
through the wheezy streets

and spreads—the Autumn
cobwebs hung

maniacal yellow.
Our bloodshot eyes

and constricted throats
are stinging, sore with it—

it covers our windshields
and house steps—

so fine a dusting
children stop and spit—

scratch their names in it.

Gray Wedding Dress
Stockton, CA 1870

100° rising hands ready the wood stove now the boilers steaming hands burning scrubbing the boards now rough soap hands raw stinging now comes the mangle wringing pins hanging comes the irons hot coal heavy hands comes scarring now aching so long doctor shirt ruffles my hands now holding this farmer gray dress comes rain now maybe the mud won't show so much

Ghost Town
Bodie, NV

Nothing prepares a man
for love's oppression—
not even the sudden apparition
of a shunned Chinese maid
in his bed, dead winter—
a century after her suicide.

It wouldn't matter
if you stopped loving me.

You would still wake
in a sweat, feel me
straddling you—ribs,
heart, lungs aching.

Look how my mouth
and tongue already press
against yours—ghost-silent
and you no longer breathing.

Chinese Dairy Hand
Lodi, 1885

        waving
        a cheese knife, comically
yelling

    Me kill you! Me kill you!

          sweat trickling

chickens flapping, children

        squealing, flushed
        out of hiding

and everyone laughing until

      the last milk can is washed

and moonlight spills
    it's sorrow—

the scent of her skin remembered—

chased nightly,
    dear opium.

Psithurism

Listen—
it once lulled me to sleep:
                      the forest
    an ocean, through
and through the open windows
        but now that I've left
the memory of it
              just keeps me awake.
Maybe it's the longing I long for—
        open windows
                swaying nights
the dark hulking trees
              bending and bowing
to the first stirrings of love.

Anniversary

Strong,
    this craggy
        cliff—

where nude oak
    twists
   twines   roots

into the cracked
    starlit rock—

look at us, love

   gripped
     and silent
each holding
    the other

  so as not to fall—

the reeling ground
    almost rising

Arthur's Drowned—

       his   body
laid   across

the stained   backseat
   tail lights   glowing

      the grave sun
still   lowering—

the horizon   the water
all   horribly   red

who can look   oh, look
everything   everything's

red

Nest

Hattie is crying
for the baby robins
she found covered in ants
last Saturday.

She would not leave
their twisted-pink bodies
(laid out for viewing
on the backyard pavers)
until we troweled
a matchbox grave in the ivy.

At her age, I also memorized
ugly deaths—fingered
dried, peeling deer skin
stuck to skulls and jaw bones
before I flung them back
to the throbbing forest.

No wonder Hattie's crying—
her small practicing hands
burying me under blankets
on her down-soft, suburban bed—

falling,
 falling,
our nested hearts,
transparent,
plunge.

Nell

has grown old.

She swells   hangs   hums
mmm—hmm bless you.

She sits by the window
in her dark Morris chair, cradles
penny-cold hands, rubs fingertips
smooth, opens her milk-blue eyes.

Nell no longer hears
rats rolling walnuts in the walls—
no longer sees the bald
light bulbs that swing.

She has two black shoes, one
metal leg brace. Six hooked canes.

Nell looks out the window—

wild oranges
drop and tumble outside.

Gobstopper

I watch his heart
    harden—
        each school day
  pushed up against the others,
layers so packed—
      it could break jaws.

If he hides it for later
    I'm afraid
        he'll forget
  he put it on the bookshelf
between Amulet and TinTin—

or worse,
        that he'll find it
    stuffed in some pocket
all-covered in lint,
    and then accidentally
      drop it—
          brittle star
exploded on the blacktop.

If only I could carry his heart
    for him   safe
      in my animal-mouth
    licked and sucked
      like a bruise—each
tempered coating
      dissolved to the last
soft, chalky center—

sugar sugar, teeth aching.

Ink Blot

When we saw the contents of the wooden box displayed on the table, we were curious. *We were!* There were old, yellowed bank statements from the 1800's. *That was interesting!* There was a personal letter and we read it, almost blushing. Other things, too. But, the dingy paper scrap blotted with William's pen ink?...well, we laughed out loud. *We couldn't stop ourselves!* Only it hurt her feelings. *We could tell!* Oh, but it was absurd, don't you see? *She held it so tenderly, with such reverence—the paper scrap!* We imagined the good doctor in his brown duster, digging his heels into the sweaty flanks of his horse, off to treat sick gold miners. *We couldn't stop ourselves!* "Christ Almighty," he muttered, turning to go.

Furniture

Strange, as if possessed—
    their carved feet

thud on wood floors
  like restless dogs.

Arthur collected the furniture—
    each mahogany piece

meant for a home
    he never built.

There should've been photographs—
    a woman at the secretary

or children lounging with books
    on the old horsehair couch.

  Arguments should have erupted
over whose turn it was

to wind the Victrola
    or set the table. But no,

  everybody knows
    he was too young

to drown. It's a grief
    we still carry—

look how we still lug
        his furniture

    house to house;
each generation

    inheriting the same
           settling sorrow, each

cumbersome heirloom
        instructing the children:

Lift with your knees! Watch the corners!
Check the water before you dive!

Rosewild

mailboxes and cotton house dresses   window screens   wood chairs   grass   spectacles   shot guns   hair pinned into tidy buns   platters   garden spigots   dogs   white roses   straw hats   books   drawers and ribbons   hard dirt paths   false teeth tomato plants   the Victrola   chickens   baby clothes   salt licks smooth braids   rust   jams and jellies   wheel barrows   glass straws   dull knives   Chinese silks   hay and sunlight   pickles apron strings   swinging gates   climbing roses   piano keys   black walnuts   the pump house   oak   suspenders   rat traps   barn green rafters   carved mahogany   slanted floors   cracked leather rakes   nests and eggs   yellow roses   tire swings   thermometers leaves   cigarettes   handkerchiefs   cats   dust and grape vines velvet   thorns   chipped saucers   pigs   wicker   coats and trousers pasture   blooms   oranges   cows   sheet music   wagon wheels glowing porch lights   button jars   bamboo   pomegranates silver hand mirrors   black widows   possum   dusk   cobwebs dark tree branches   fog   fences   porcelain dolls   perfume tricycles   pink roses   swallows and poppies   wedding rings irrigation ditches   metal buckets   blue sky   dents   crates moonlight   stacked wood   peaches   ladders and pressed glass figs falling   pink naked ladies   the secret staircase   cookie tins   sheep   clotheslines   stars   ink bottles   sprinklers   soft lamp light   bedspreads   wash tubs   potato chips   cake stands soda pop   creaks and doors   wind-up clocks   the claw foot tub carpet   red roses   dry toast   grizzly bear skins   top hats   ghosts

Pregnant

      the acacia is singing
trumpeting
bloom

and little Ruby's in heat—
   sniffed out and humped
 in the pod heavy
shade

     then, there is
this wild moon
       fat yellow
and balmy

listen,

I'll say to him,
changing

Pancreatic Cancer

Auntie Pam gathered her things,
spread them around her quilted bed

and watched us carefully pick and choose—
dust floating in the windowed sunlight.

We ate Mediterranean sandwiches from *Panera*,
placed small vases and teacups, glass straws

and hair pins into awkward piles, watched her
carefully nibble a sodium-packed pickle spear.

From her: a tiny box I now fill
with my children's lost baby teeth.

Rattling and blood-crusted, they are
not as perfect as you'd think.

Don't tell Ben about the pickle,
she said, perking up.

Aquafina©

Hunched naked, I'm retching
into the blue soup pot
Jay placed at the foot of our bed.

Holding back my hair,
my moonstruck body, he's awed
by your force.

No bigger than a thought—you
already bring me to this ground,
wincing and grinning

how lucky I am, how
I want you, how can

bottled water taste bad?

Moving Virginia
to Senior Housing

It's like that morning
of the big storm
at the wooden Live Oak School
when the cooped up children
gathered on the front porch
breathing out clouds
in the wet air.

The wind gusted up—
catching the huge oak
that had stood for years
on the corner of Cherokee Lane.

It's leafless branches
trembled and shook
until it finally lifted out
of the soaked ground
and stayed like that—
suspended—
dirt clods dropping,
the splayed roots exposed

and as shocked
as the children who saw it.

Tuber

Sleepless and hungry
I stand barefoot in dark kitchen: eat

from recycled yogurt container
one organic homegrown baby red

leftover wrinkled potato and
congratulate myself—this moment

I waste nothing.   2:03 a.m.

Heather Angier has an MFA in English and Creative Writing from Mills College. She is the author of the chapbook *Crooked* (Dancing Girl Press, 2012) and currently lives in Oakland, California.

hangier@sbcglobal.net

www.ingramcontent.com/pod-product-compliance
Lightning Source LLC
Chambersburg PA
CBHW060226050426
42446CB00013B/3184